THE VALUE OF HONESTY

The Story of Confucius

VALUE COMMUNICATIONS, INC.
PUBLISHERS
LA JOLLA, CALIFORNIA

THE VALUE OF HONESTY

The Story of
Confucius

BY SPENCER JOHNSON, M.D.

THE DANBURY PRESS

The Value of Honesty is part of the ValueTales series.

The Value of Honesty text copyright © 1979 by Spencer Johnson, M.D.
Illustrations copyright © 1979 by Value Communications, Inc.

First Edition
Manufactured in the United States of America
For information write to: ValueTales, P.O. Box 1012
La Jolla, CA 92038

Library of Congress Cataloging in Publication Data

Johnson, Spencer.
    The value of honesty.

    (ValueTales)
    SUMMARY: A biography of the Chinese philosopher
and teacher emphasizing his ideas about the value of honesty.
    1.   Confucius—Juvenile literature.2.   Philosophers—
China—Biography—Juvenile literature. 3.   Honesty—
Juvenile literature. [1. Confucius. 2. Philosophers.
3. Honesty] I. Title.
B128.C8J63   299'.5126'3 [B] [92]   79-4351

ISBN 0-916392-36-8

This tale is about an honest person, Confucius. The story that follows is based on events in his life. More historical facts about Confucius can be found on page 63.

Once upon a time...

many, many years ago, a little boy named Confucius lived with his mother and father in the province of Lu in the far-off land of China.

Like most children, Confucius liked to play and dance and laugh and sing songs. He also liked it when he was with his parents.

The boy's parents thought Confucius was a very special child, but that is not surprising. Parents often think that their children are remarkable.

What *is* surprising is the way that the boy's father spoke to him.

Confucius was only three years old when his father called him one day.

Confucius went and stood at his father's knee. His father said, "I believe that when you grow up, you will become a very wise person, and you will help many people with your wisdom."

His father could see that Confucius did not understand, and he smiled. "You are still very young," he said, "but when you think more about what I have said, you will understand."

Confucius did think about it, and he decided that when he was a little older, he would ask his father to explain about wisdom. Before he could do this, however, his father, who was very, very old, became ill and died.

"I miss Father," he said to his mother. "And I wonder why he thought I would grow up to be a wise person," said Confucius.

"Perhaps he said that because he loved you," said his mother. "And perhaps he thought that if you believed it, you would make it come true."

"But how can I make it come true?" asked young Confucius. "I do not even know what a wise person is."

Confucius sat by himself and thought about this.

And then something happened!

Suddenly it seemed that a little old man appeared, quite magically, right before his eyes. He was indeed a little man—only six inches tall!

"You seem troubled, my young friend," said the little man.

Confucius laughed. He knew that there really was no such thing as a six-inch man. He had made up the small person out of his own imagination. But Confucius was puzzled about wisdom, and it was comforting to have someone to talk to, even if he was just talking to himself.

"Hello, little old man," said Confucius.

"You may call me Sage," the little man said.

"Sage?" echoed Confucius. "What a strange name!"

"Not really," said the tiny man. "A very wise person is often called a sage, and I am a very wise person!"

Confucius' eyes brightened. "You are wise? Wonderful! Can you teach me to be wise, too?"

"I can do better than that, young friend," said the little man. "I can help you to teach yourself."

"I'm ready!" exclaimed Confucius. "What do I do first?"

"You begin by learning what other people already know," said Sage. "You can do that by reading good books."

Now in Confucius' day, books were actually written by hand on bamboo slats, which were then tied together with leather straps. Confucius was so eager to become wise, as his father had predicted, that he read his books again and again. His poor mother had to keep replacing the worn-out leather straps.

"Reading is a very good way to become wise," said Sage, "but not all wisdom is found in books. You can also learn much by watching and listening to people. Try to understand what they are thinking and feeling. Even if people don't tell you how they feel, you will know if you watch them closely."

Confucius followed Sage's advice, and he found that he did learn by watching and listening.

"Perhaps I am on my way to becoming wise," said Confucius.

Confucius might have been wiser than most boys his age, but he certainly was not wealthier. He started to work when he was quite young, and one of his first jobs was tending animals.

"You're very good at that," said Sage, after Confucius had been on the job for some time. "The animals look so healthy, and the herd has grown much larger since you began to care for it. How do you do it, my young friend?"

"Very easily," said Confucius. "I feed the animals and run with them and care for them the way I'd like someone to care for me if I were an animal."

Sage wasn't the only one who noticed the change in the herd. The man who owned the animals was so pleased that he gave Confucius a bigger, more important job.

"You may measure grain into sacks," he told Confucius, "and then sell the sacks to the townspeople."

"You can make some extra money for yourself," whispered another man who also sold grain in the market. "When you measure the grain into the sacks, don't put in the full measure. No one will be the wiser."

"That would be dishonest," said Confucius. "I would not like to be treated dishonestly, so I will not treat others that way."

15

"Young Confucius is very honest," said the people who came to buy grain. "He never gives us less than we pay for."

"I can use someone who is honest," said a storekeeper who lived nearby, and he offered Confucius the job of managing his shop.

"How great!" said Confucius to Sage. "Now I can watch many people, and listen to them, and I can learn a great deal."

"Very true," said Sage, "and don't forget that people will also be watching *you!*"

Confucius didn't forget. He always treated the customers as he would have liked them to treat him, and he always gave people the correct change.

"He is an honest man," the people said. "He is wise, too. When he isn't working in the shop, he is reading a book. He knows a great deal, that young fellow."

Confucius' good reputation grew until one day a rich man came into the shop and asked if Confucius would teach his son.

"I admire your wisdom and your honesty," said the man. "I would like my son to learn what you know."

What do you think Confucius did when he heard this?

Why he became a teacher—and such a good teacher that soon he had many pupils.

"I will open a school," he said to Sage, "but I want to be fair. I don't want to teach only the sons of rich men. I would like to teach everyone who wants to learn—even the sons of poor men. And I have a plan that will help me do it!"

Confucius then went to the fathers of his wealthy pupils. "I will charge you a large amount of money to teach your children," he said. "Then I can afford to teach poor children for no money at all. Now tell me honestly how much money you have, and I will tell you what you must pay for your son's schooling."

The wealthy men did not like this. They did not see why the sons of poor men should have an education. But they wanted Confucius to teach their boys and so, one by one, they told him how much money they had.

The fathers of Confucius' poorer pupils told him, too, although some of them were ashamed to admit how very poor they were.

Confucius then told each father what he must pay, and at last the school was ready to begin. There were only boys in the school, for in those days girls were not allowed to have an education.

And what do you think was the first lesson Confucius taught those boys?

It was a lesson about two very important words.

"How many of you heard your father answer my question about his wealth?" Confucius asked his pupils.

Many of the boys, both rich and poor, raised their hands. Even the son of the powerful duke who ruled the province was in the class, and he raised his hand, too.

"What did your fathers have to do before they answered my question?" asked Confucius, in his soft tone. "With whom did they have to be honest before they could be honest with me?"

The boys thought about this, and then one of them said, "They had to be honest with themselves."

"Ah, Yu, that is correct," said Confucius happily. Then he asked another question, for that is how Confucius taught—by asking questions.

"If I tell you that integrity comes first and honesty comes second, and that both words mean being truthful, can you tell me what the words mean?"

Sage smiled, for he knew the answer to Confucius' question. Do you know the answer?

The boys in the school had to think about it. After a few moments one of the students, the son of the Duke of Lu, raised his hand. "I think that integrity is telling the truth to yourself. Then honesty means telling the truth to someone else."

"Exactly!" cried Confucius. "That is just what the words mean! If some of your fathers decided not to tell the truth about their wealth, I might not know. But they would know that they had not acted with integrity, and perhaps this might make them unhappy."

Confucius saw then that two of the students in the back of the class were not paying attention. He frowned, but he did not shout or scold. Instead he quietly told the two boys to leave. "I will teach anyone who really wants to learn," he said, "but I will not force anyone to listen."

The boys left the class, and so they did not see what happened next.

Confucius knew that some people learn best by example, so he went to the front of the class.

"Watch this!" he whispered to Sage. Then he held a vase up in one hand so that all the boys could see it. In the other hand he had an apple. As the students watched, he dropped the apple into the vase and put the vase on the ground.

"The boy who can get the apple out of the vase may eat the apple," said he.

24

One of the boys was quite hungry, and he hurried forward and put his hand into the narrow neck of the vase. He seized the apple and tried to pull it out, but he couldn't.

"My hand is stuck!" he cried.

"You cannot get the apple out unless you let go of it," said Confucius.

The boy did not want to let go of the apple, but at last he did. He took his hand out of the vase and looked puzzled.

Can you guess of a way to get the apple out of the vase?

25

Confucius picked the vase off the ground and turned it upside down. The apple fell out into his hand. The boys all laughed. It was so simple.

"But it is not as simple as it looks," said Confucius, holding up the apple. "It is often difficult to let go of a thing. But if you see that by holding on to a thing you are keeping yourself from getting what you want, then you should let go. If you are doing something wrong, you must stop doing it. If you are being dishonest with yourself or others, you must stop that dishonesty. Only then will you reach your goal."

"I have never seen anyone teach like this," Sage whispered into Confucius' ear. "The prophecy your father made about you is coming true. I am sure of it!"

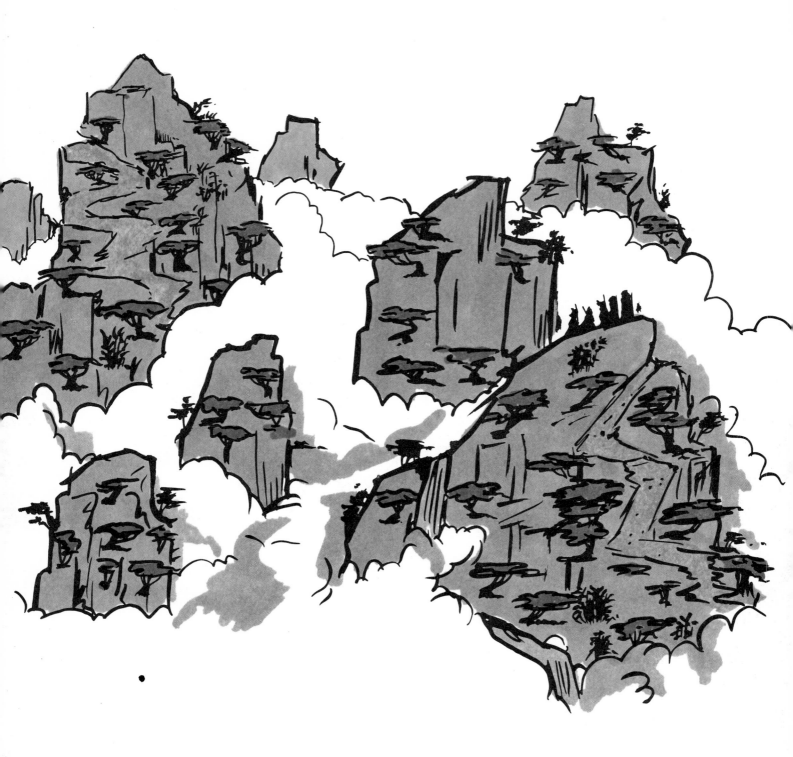

Soon there were many people who looked to Confucius as a great teacher, and not all of them were children. Some lived out in the distant forests where there was no school. Whenever Confucius learned about these people, he would go to them and talk with them about wisdom and virtue and happiness.

In those days, most people traveled by foot, so Confucius walked great distances. Of course this took a great deal of time, so Confucius decided that he would teach as he walked along. Quite naturally, the people who followed Confucius to hear what he said were called followers.

Usually it was peaceful and quiet along Confucius' route, but one day, as he was walking along, there was a horrible growling and screaming in a jungle clearing nearby.

"Look!" cried Sage, and he pointed to an old woman who crouched beside the body of a young man and wept and wailed.

"Beware!" warned one of Confucius' followers. "I saw a tiger running off into the jungle!"

What do you think had happened?

"He killed my son!" cried the old woman. "The tiger killed my son!" She sobbed with the grief of a broken heart. "It was in this very spot that a tiger killed my husband! And before that, my father was killed by a tiger!"

"But why do you stay in such a place?" Confucius asked the woman. "Do you not fear and hate the tiger who has taken the ones you love away from you?"

The woman nodded. "Of course I fear the tiger. But I am more afraid of what might happen to me if I moved away. At least the people here are kind and honest."

"I see," said Confucius, and after the woman left he said to his followers, "Think about what you have just seen. Then ask yourself what people fear more—fierce animals or cruel, dishonest people."

Like most good teachers, Confucius was also a good student. So he was ready to listen when Sage, who was really Confucius' own inner self, suggested that he should go to the distant city of Loyang to study at the fine library there.

At that time China was divided into many provinces, and each one was ruled by a noble called a duke. Confucius asked for help from the Duke of Lu to go to Loyang. He was provided with a cart, and set out with two of his followers.

"Now you can study and think," said Sage, "and become an even wiser man."

Confucius studied in Loyang for several years. He read many books in the wonderful library there, and he learned to play a musical instrument and to sing more than 300 songs.

"You are wise to study and enjoy music, my friend," said Sage. "It is so restful."

"It is," agreed Confucius. "It can be difficult when I am first learning a new piece of music. But once I have learned it, the music makes me feel calm and peaceful."

In time, Confucius began his return journey to Lu. Of course Sage went with him, and so did the two followers who had come with him to study at Loyang. The three men traveled for several days, and at last they found themselves near a city that Confucius knew well.

They stopped to rest outside the city wall, and Confucius pointed to a place where there was a break in the wall. "When I visited this city last," he said, "I entered through that break in the wall."

Several townspeople were nearby, and they were startled when they heard this. "Once an evil man named Yang Ho entered the city through this break in the wall," said one of them.

"This stranger looks like Yang Ho," said another.

The townspeople then hurried to tell the police that the cruel outlaw named Yang Ho was resting near the city wall, and that he could be captured and punished for his crimes.

While Confucius rested, the police began to surround him.

Do you know what happened then?

Confucius was seized by the police and thrown into a dark and dirty prison.

At first Confucius was afraid. He felt very much alone. But then he reminded himself that he was not really alone. He had Sage, who always said pleasant things because he was Confucius' own good thoughts. Just the same, it wasn't at all comfortable in that prison.

"I wish that Yang Ho had learned never to do to others what he would not want them to do to Yang Ho," said Confucius. "If he had, I might not be in this place today."

"You will not be here long," Sage assured him.

Indeed, Confucius' followers had run to tell the citizens of Lu that the great teacher was in prison. Many people who knew Confucius hurried to the prison to identify him as an honorable man who should be treated with respect. Of course the police officials released Confucius immediately.

"And what have you learned from this?" Confucius asked his followers when they were again on their way home.

"When people know that you behave well," said one young man, "they, in turn, will behave well toward you."

Confucius and his followers were nearly home when they saw a royal messenger approaching.

"My lord," said the messenger, bowing to Confucius, "the Duke of Lu asks that you come to the palace."

Confucius agreed to follow the messenger to the palace. Sage was terribly excited. He knew that the person who was then the Duke of Lu had once been a boy in Confucius' class. "I wonder why he wants to see you," said Sage.

Confucius and Sage soon learned why. The young duke wanted Confucius to advise him on how best to govern the province.

"I will be happy to advise you," Confucius told the duke. "I have always wanted to see my ideas put to practical use, so that I could help more people."

So the Duke of Lu began to do as Confucius advised. He behaved properly and honestly, and he respected other people.

And then what do you think happened?

Because their ruler was honest with his subjects and treated them well, the people of Lu became more honest with one another. The merchants did not cheat their customers and the laborers were not idle on their jobs. Roads and bridges were repaired so it was easier for people to travel. More food was grown, so the people were better nourished. They spoke kindly to one another, and they felt better because of it.

In time the bandits were driven out of the mountains, and Lu became a very safe place to live. Everyone, young and old, rich and poor, was treated fairly in the courts. Honesty was rewarded and dishonesty was punished.

The people were happy to live in such a place.

41

Often the people of Lu stopped to talk with one another of their new way of life.

"Isn't it wonderful?" they would say. "Life works so much better when we all behave in an honorable way. What a good thing that Confucius is advising our duke. And the duke is wise to follow his advice."

42

And so, for three years, things went on very happily in Lu. But elsewhere people were not happy. In Ch'i, which was the province next to Lu, the ruler was neither honest nor kind. He made himself rich by taxing the peasants, and he gave them nothing in return for their taxes.

"Be careful!" warned the ruler's friends. "Your people are beginning to talk against you. They want you to be more like the Duke of Lu."

The Duke of Ch'i scowled. "I do not intend to change my ways," he said. "I would rather the Duke of Lu changed his—and he would if we could get rid of Confucius. He is the one who is causing all the trouble!"

And the Duke of Ch'i thought of a way he might bring this about.

He sent the Duke of Lu a present of 85 beautiful dancers and 125 wonderful horses. "It is a gift," he said, "to show my admiration for you."

Of course this was a lie. He only wanted the Duke of Lu to ignore Confucius and spend all of his time having fun.

The wicked plan succeeded. The Duke of Lu became much too involved in entertaining himself to worry about his people—or about Confucius.

"What will you do now?" Sage asked Confucius. "The duke won't listen to you. He doesn't even want to see you."

Confucius sighed, for he knew what the answer must be. "I cannot force anyone to be wise," he said. "We will leave this province."

Quietly, Confucius left the palace of Lu. As he began to walk through the countryside, he looked back over his shoulder. He was hoping that the duke would send a messenger after him. But no messenger came. The Duke of Lu was busy enjoying his wonderful gifts from the Duke of Ch'i. He wasn't thinking about anyone's feelings but his own.

Confucius thought about the other neighboring provinces. "Perhaps we will go to Wei," he said. "Or perhaps the Duke of Sung would make us welcome."

But as Confucius and his friends wandered in the countryside, trying to decide which would be the best place for them to go, they looked back and saw that there were soldiers following them.

"That is the army of the Duke of Ch'i," said Sage. "For a long time he has hated you because you believe that a ruler should be virtuous and honest— which he is not. He is afraid that his people will rise up against him. And now I'm afraid that his army will kill you!"

"Perhaps they will, Sage," said Confucius.

Then, since it was beginning to rain, Confucius took shelter under a great tree, and he waited.

The followers of Confucius were very upset. Some of them wanted to remain with their teacher and others wanted to run away. "We will be killed if we stay," they said. "What can we do against an army?"

Confucius saw that they were concerned, and he called his three favorite students to him.

"When you see that your teacher has not the power of a ruler, and his ideas are not listened to, and he is about to be killed, do you think that he is a wise man?"

The first two students were confused and frightened.

"I don't know," said one.

"I'm not sure," said another.

Do you know what the third one said?

He looked at Confucius with great respect. "Your task is to tell the truth," he said. "You must be honest with yourself and with others, and do what you feel is right. If the truth is not accepted by other people, *they* are the ones who are wrong. You cannot change the truth just so that you will be accepted by those people. If you do, you will be unhappy."

Confucius smiled. "You have learned your lessons well," he said. "Very well indeed."

Then, as the rain continued to pour down, Confucius sat out in the open and played music and sang. He knew he was in danger, but he was happy. He knew that he was a good and honest man, and even if the soldiers killed him, they could not destroy this truth.

But the soldiers did not kill Confucius, for he had many friends. It was to one of these friends that a follower of Confucius ran for help.

This friend was a powerful man who had soldiers of his own. When he heard that a hostile army threatened Confucius, he called his generals and sent them to rescue the great teacher.

When the army of the evil duke saw the other soldiers approaching, they ran away. They had planned to kill Confucius, but they were not ready for a fair fight.

Some people think that Confucius was always perfect—always polite and honest. Confucius and Sage knew this wasn't so. Confucius was like all of us. He made mistakes now and then.

Once, when he was living in a small hut in the jungle, a man whom he did not like came to see him.

"I really don't want to see that man," said Confucius. "In fact, I dislike him so much that I will be quite rude to him."

54

Confucius then told one of his followers to tell the man that he was not at home. Once having done this, he sat in his hut, played some music, and sang very loudly so that the man would know that he *was* home.

"You lied," said Sage, "and you hurt that man's feelings."

Confucius knew it, and the more he thought about it the more unhappy he felt.

"Never mind," said Sage. "Worrying won't help. Just try to learn from your mistakes."

As he grew older, Confucius learned more and more and more. He learned from reading, from watching, and from listening. He even learned from his mistakes.

After he had wandered through China for fourteen years, Confucius was called home again to the province of Lu. Again he took his place in the royal court, and again the duke listened to his wise advice.

By now, Confucius looked very much like Sage. And if Sage still whispered into the mind of the wise old man, well, no one noticed. For in fact Confucius had become a sage.

57

"I have learned much by reading books," said Confucius to Sage. "Perhaps at last I am wise enough to begin to write a book of my own."

"I think you are," said Sage. "What will you call your book?"

"I will call it *Spring and Autumn*," answered Confucius. "It will be the history of the province of Lu. I will write down what has happened here for the last 250 years. I will point out what I think was wise and what was unwise, so that others may read and learn from my book."

"But he knows so much," said Confucius' followers. "He will never be able to write it all down. We must help."

So the students who surrounded Confucius listened to him and wrote down much of what he said. Today, much of what we know about this great teacher, who lived 2,500 years ago, is because of what was written down by his followers.

One of the things they wrote down was this: When each person learns to be honest with himself, he will like himself. And when many people do this, the world will be a better place to live in.

Many things have changed in China since the time of Confucius. Today it is a modern land. In some ways the people are different. But in many ways they are still the same. They still talk about Confucius—even though he lived so many years ago. Perhaps they know he was right.

Do you think Confucius was right? Do you believe that being honest with yourself and others helps you feel good about yourself?

Only you can decide about the value of honesty in your own life. But whatever you decide, let's hope that it gives you a good feeling about yourself.

Just like it did for our good friend Confucius.

The End

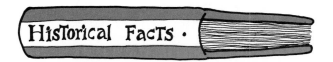

Confucius was born more than 2,500 years ago in the state of Lu, which is now the province of Shantung in China. He was the first and only son of Shuh-liang Heih, commandant of the district of Tsow, who was more than 70 when Confucius was born.

Some scholars and historians have regarded Confucius as a very holy man. It is doubtful, however, that Confucius was religious in the traditional sense. Instead, he believed that life's purpose was that people attain perfection within themselves. His teachings were about four basic subjects: literature, human conduct, being one's true self, and honesty in social relationships.

The heart of Confucius' teachings was what he called "shu," which is the same as our Golden Rule. Repeatedly he said, "Do not do unto others what you would not have others do unto you."

During his years of study and teaching, Confucius traveled widely throughout China. Then, when he was 52, he was called to office in Lu, his native state, and made governor of Chung-tu. His social reforms would be considered advanced even today. He not only fed the poor, he assigned different foods to the young and old. He organized labor, allotting easier tasks to the weak and more difficult ones to the strong. While he was in office, communications were improved, roads and bridges were repaired, and the outlaws who roamed the mountains were rooted out. People were freed from oppression and made equal in the eyes of justice.

As Confucius' fame grew, more and more people wanted to study with him. Once, he taught poetry, history, ceremonies, and music to about 3,000 pupils. His standards were so high, though, that he felt that only 72 of his students had mastered these subjects.

Confucius strongly believed that the first duty of a ruler was to be virtuous, and that this would ensure harmony among the people. However, except for his post as governor of Chung-tu in Lu, Confucius never succeeded in attaining a position in which he could put his ideas about moral government into practice. But as he grew old, he took joy in seeing many of his students, to whom he had taught his moral principles, attain positions of power.

CONFUCIUS (K'UNG FU-TZE)
551 B.C. – 478 B.C.

In 478 B.C., Confucius died at the age of 73. He was buried in Lu on the River Sze. More than 100 families decided that they wanted to be near the great teacher, and they built homes not far from Confucius' grave. People came there to study and think, and to talk with one another. For more than 200 years the families of Confucius' disciples stayed on, and to this day the area is known as K'ungli, China, or K'ung's Village—the Village of Kung the Philosopher.

Why K'ung's Village? Because K'ung was the true name of the great philosopher. Confucius is the way it was translated into Latin, and then English. It means K'ung fu-tzu—"the philosopher K'ung."

During the last twenty centuries there have been many other great Chinese philosophers, but none has had as much impact on the world as Confucius did. Although he was not religious, his ideas about morality became a religion—called Confucianism—which has been the only state religion of China. And this man, who never claimed to be more than an imperfect human, has been regarded almost as a god. Certainly he would be proud to know that his teachings have been so widely respected; but probably he would not at all like the idea of himself as a god.

63